An Ark *of Sorts*

Also by Celia Gilbert

Bonfire
Alice James Books

Queen of Darkness
Viking Press

An Ark *of Sorts*

poems

CELIA GILBERT

ALICE JAMES BOOKS
FARMINGTON, MAINE

The Jane Kenyon Chapbook Award Series #1

Cover and book design by Elizabeth Knox.
Cover art: Pierre Bonnard, "Maisons dans la cour," pastel.
Courtesy of the Trustees of the Museum of Fine Arts, Boston, MA.
Printed by Thomson-Shore, Inc., Dexter, MI.

The text of this book is set in Sabon.
This book is printed on acid-free paper.

Library of Congress Cataloging-in-Publication Data
Gilbert, Celia
An ark of sorts : poems / by Celia Gilbert.
p. cm.— (The Jane Kenyon chapbook award series : #1)
ISBN 1-882295-18-8
PS3557.I335A89 1998
811'.54—dc21 97-39063
CIP

THIRD PRINTING

Alice James Books are published by
The Alice James Poetry Cooperative, Inc.
University of Maine at Farmington
98 Main Street, Farmington, ME 04938

For all of us

Contents

All of us are creatures of the day;
the rememberer and the remembered alike.

—Marcus Aurelius

Dust

The plane trees turn gray,
an empty Paris in August.
Foreigners ask foreigners for directions.
Apartments to rent offer shabby bombast:
fake antiques, threadbare needlepoint,
freckled plates.
The hot avenues and dim rooms
spell drought into my palm.

At Napoleon's tomb, his son's
empty, marble cradle.
The children think we'll never find a place to live.
Home was all of us together. We're exiles now.

Sky

Seven floors up, our rooms.
We've leased a bit of sky
and tiny balconies where we can lean
like passengers on a sea voyage
moving without volition.
Across the air our neighbors,
La Bohème, wild gestures and quarrels.
Each day they hang their caged birds outside
above the geraniums on the sill.
At lunch she fries something in a flat pan
and he stands behind her
slowly caressing her back.
I want their life.

Our Lady

A small green sign near granite steps
points to the Memorial to the Deportation.
Our Lady, Notre-Dame, here is where
you turned your back, this quiet space
behind your cathedral,
where the Seine
renamed herself Lethe.

In the crypt, darkness until
shards of light reveal
words of dead poets
and the names of death camps
engraved behind iron grilles.

Against the lapping water I hear
the shuffling lines of families,
the mothers and children,
taking those first steps into the fog.

I imagine us, her hand clutching mine,
as it did when she went for radiation,
fearful but trusting.

Bedtime

On these bedroom walls, blue and white rows
of shepherd and shepherdess keep watch.
This used to be my favorite time,
listening to the three of them in turn, their faces
flushed with the unfolding of their day.
I think I was like a god then
feeding on the savor of their stories.
Now at their bedsides, in the moment between
what he and she tell me and the space where nothing
will or can be said, my embrace
carries the pollution of despair.

At the Sidewalk Café

The waiter smiles,
the children dispel his surliness;
to have children is to belong to the family.
We sun ourselves in little wrought-iron chairs
at a round table with spindly wire legs.
The waiter clacks down ham sandwiches,
and glasses of foaming fresh squeezed lemonade.
The children, ravenous, begin but
an old woman dressed in long black skirts
stops at the curb, her ravaged, rouged face thrown back,
eyes half-shut in pleasure,
lips trembling in distress. The children
see it first and blush—the long rivulet
of yellow between her shoes.

Washing My Hair

When I rinse, strands fall out,
twining around my fingers,
like drowning things. Fear, as in the dream
of my teeth crumbling, here, awake,
body shutting down,
the way a parched tree shuts down,
letting everything go but the necessary.

Holding On

Because the dead have no memory
we must always be remembering for them.
You learn now to live under water.
Even if you grow pale with longing
for sunlight and sunsets of violet,
you must float with the currents and be of them—

and it is comforting here without the treacherous,
shifting temperatures of the earth world.
Some would call it dark
but I say no: here shines
all the light I need. Here everything exists,
though it cannot grow.

The Balcony

An ark of sorts, the balcony
bears me between earth and air
indifferent now
to raven, rainbow, dove.

Seen from above,
people move head first, then feet.
In the UNESCO garden, a stone woman
lies on her side, frozen
in O's of emptiness.

I walk from inside to outside
looking for a space, a place.
A railing keeps me from the street.
To go out: words of freedom,
but duty, *devoir,* is an absolute:
my task, to see, *voir*
for her, to *be* for both of us, we creatures
of the day.

Market Day

On Tuesdays I go to the *marché.*
My shopping cart squeaks along
between the trestle tables.
Behind them men and women
with chapped hands clamor
to catch my eye while I admire
pyramids of blood oranges and leeks,
white-legged like fillies, piled near
tightly wrapped nosegays
of parsley, chives, and thyme,
and tiny peeled potatoes the color of ivory.
Mushrooms sprout in sandy boxes,
some with black gills, or orange-red ones
called *pleurotes,* the word
that makes me cry, *pleurer.*

After I've put the food away,
I'll throw myself on the bed, dressed,
weeping, and sleep for hours
until the children arrive from school.
Then I'll leap up, guilty, abandoning her
as they come running in,
fearful of some new loss.

November

I have never lived alone.
Child. Child-wife. Child-mother.
My Vietnamese friend, until she came to Paris,
had never been in a room
with fewer than three people.

November, the wanderer's month.
Even a dog, especially a dog they say,
can bring a speechless person back to words.
Oh miracle of the unstinting,
the outpouring of breath in the palm,
the look intimate as an angel's
that seems to read us and forgive.

But I have never loved a dog. Am I too proud?
November turns its back on the harvest.
I feel and fear the oncoming cold.
Daughter, you hold my hand, but your sister—
how can I accept that she has let me go?

The sound of buses—
the little bell the conductor rings
to make them cough and set off once more.

Teatime

Leaden sky of an autumn afternoon.
The cherries swell in their lucent jelly,
nested in fluted tarts alongside the Napoleons.
Napoléon, the man who died of arsenic slowly,
the conqueror, the killer, canonized in cake.
Sic semper tyrannis!
Sallow with true Parisian pallor, the children
arrive from school, fling down their satchels,
but today, breathless,
you throw yourself into my lap sobbing
while your brother averts his eyes.
Your friend Claudine's curly-haired little sister
came to school. "But I don't have *my* sister anymore."
Last month you turned eight. When I was your age
I cried because I had to wear glasses.
I can't bear your sorrow.
I dry your tears, point to the table.

Through Glass

The sun, a pale insomniac, struggles
through frosted panes of kitchen glass.
What had he said, innocent ten-year-old,
that made my sobs begin? My mouth sags.
He's looking down at me bent over the sink
in my old green bathrobe.
I know I should stop; I feel his panic. "Stop!" he says.
"You might go crazy."
He said, that first night when I came to put him to bed,
"This is too terrible. We mustn't think about it any more."
He looks so much like the sister he loved.
Will we ever talk?
"Make sure you eat," he says, picking up his school bag.

Night

The children sleep.
Behind me on the mantelpiece,
reflected from the darkness of the window,
a Chinese traveler with a broad-brimmed hat
slouches on his terra-cotta donkey;
my face is his worried moon.
Stroking the worn green leather of the desk,
I try to write letters.
I had good friends, I think,
but what are they to me? When death happened,
I embarked on a sleepless journey like an Egyptian,
eyes painted open on the coffin
that holds me, such a sarcophagus
as the children and I saw in the Louvre,
with bold red and black bands
and prayers of magic that scaled its sides.
Mail from home arrives infrequently.
How difficult it is to communicate
with someone of another world.

Reading Madame de Sévigné

Your daughter, married, departed.
Daughter whose absence
you chronicled for her:
I looked for you in every room,
step on the stair, nook of the garden...
A thousand letters you wrote
to woo her, to seduce her back.

Like me, avowed idolater: *I think of you incessantly*
as the devout think habitually of God.
Your stiff calligraphy
slanted in the hurricane winds of
your passionate wit.

Focused through a magnifying glass, the sun
transforms ordinary light into fire.
Only while writing to her
were you truly alive.

Marquise, put your hand over mine.
On my blank page
write out with me that time of dusk
you feared and named
between the dog and the wolf.

Bread

Hands reach, seize, slice, and prepare.
The feel of veined cabbage,
grit of potato peels, luscious soft
of pig fat, dimpled scrolls
of orange rind.

Hands move the dishes to the table,
remove the dishes to the sink.
Standing, waiting, empty,
back and forth, confined,
I mark minutes without sums.
Then the spirit, blinded, rises,
resists knowing itself chained.
I go round the grindstone reducing grain
to something that could be bread.

Thaw

January's unnatural spring brings out mothers.
Navy-blue baby carriages on high wheels
glide like water spiders around the garden
of the Palais Royale.
Small pecking sounds of pigeons on the gravel
alternate with a fountain's purl.
I'm watching a man stuffed into an overcoat
poke along with a black umbrella.
He talks to himself in two voices,
one high and irritated,
the other rumbling and violent.
His coat like a pupa's case readies to split.
The mothers pull their children close.

Unprepared

Unprepared
for doctors and their denials;
for a starving child,
her old woman's eyes.

Nowhere

A frieze of gurneys against the wall,
whey-faced men and women wait for radiation to flood
their bones. The sheet slips back from gnarled feet
and hands lift swollen veins, blue ropes climbing
to nowhere hearts. In these cold corridors,
I stand helpless, all lost
before my disbelieving eyes.

By Candlelight

How could I believe
such a small thing as hope
could keep me warm so long,
or, burning within you
as the morphine cradled you down
day by day, keep you
until the last sigh blew it out?

When

When the tablecloth and all the settings
fall to the floor, everything in a heap,
the table hard and bare.

When you sprawl headlong, hear a bone break.

When a window shatters and a spider's web
traps your face.

Until Now

The light fell on your rigid
form. Until now I held you
and did not, would not, place
a last kiss because I knew not to do
a last anything. *Life was each small now*
next to its exactly same neighbor.
Until that now
in the ride to the hospital when
time changed as ice to vapor, and it was then.
What was our sin,
for surely we were without guilt, ignorant,
until then?

Translated

The bereaved wore white. What was there to mourn?

If the message true: Summerland, flowers, sky.
God's call, Come home.

Not "Died," "Translated."

Giving away the clothes, the toys:
emptying the closet.

Curtains drawn, eyes closed, around the table,
held hands and heard *the rapping.*

Monologue

The fork goes so, the knife here,
and spoon to the right of the plate.

Wanting revenge, not resignation

Then, the napkin to the left of the
fork. Pull the tablecloth straight.

Wanting to lie, wanting to betray

The wine glasses to the right of the dish—
they sparkle diligently.

Breaking the hold of duty and goodness

Take this small brush and pan for sweeping
the crumbs from the table.

Flight

The taxi drives off.
I watch from the balcony
how he turns to wave, on to his other life,
his work that never stopped,
not even when she was dying.

Who can parse suffering or loss?
There can never be equality of grief.
We don't speak of my feelings
or his, no moments of sharing
when I can rest from
keeping her memory alive.

A solitary walk along the quais,
students swarming into the sun.
How sensuous, liberty!

The trees begin to work a lace
against the sky, the evanescent filigree
before summer's screen.

I remember us lying on the spring earth
while we watched the changing clouds.

Now in his arms, I imagine someone else,
betrayal the coward's way in an erotic fugue.

Fragments

A weekend in the country
without the children.
Alone—for the first time in years—
a silence like two people
suddenly gone deaf.
In the empty inn tonight
the waiter had nothing to do
but fill our glasses.
Drunk, we touched one another as if
there could be a new beginning.

I lie beside you, throwing off the quilt,
studying your body in the moonlight.
Outside, the cathedral clock strikes two
and footsteps stumble over the cobbles.

The cracked bidet, the cheap hotel
in Paris—the first time.

In the Gods

Julius Katchen's last concert.
We sit in the gods, the cheap seats,
the stage a far-off circle of light.

Sixteen years ago, in cousin Rachel's kitchen,
Katchen taught me how to make
French scrambled eggs:
immense quantities of butter,
coddled under the lowest heat possible.
He was plump and funny,
no more romantic than a tailor, I thought.

The audience knows he is dying.
The Steinway opens like an ebony butterfly.
He appears, frail, framed
in the applause, flicking aside his coattails;
sits, hands poised, then takes us up with him
into the work, the human work
of being greater than ourselves.
And when he bends low over the keys,
it is your face I see, husband,
bending over me. All these years,
how delicious those eggs.
I have never forgotten the patience, the care.

Tides

The waiter, with his short beaked knife,
opens the oysters, their shells small atolls
rough with extinct volcanoes.
Spring time. Venus time. Oyster fruit
floats suspended, gray-white, in
crystalline pools. See ourselves
reflected in the beveled mirror
on Thonet chairs whose gracious curves
recall a Degas woman stepping in the bath,
returning to her element.
When the oysters begin their slide, I shiver.
Is it a full mouth pursing, a throat contracting,
or the feeling I've swallowed the moon?

The Secret

Your head, bent to the keyboard
these many months, reveals
a white path that zigzags
between shining, disheveled braids.
The metronome: click, clack, distract, distract.
Only Agnès when she comes to clean
can bring order to your unruly hair.

You have a crush on Mademoiselle your teacher;
she praises your flexible hands,
but you do not love to practice.

One and two, one and two,
one and two and three...

"The art," says Mademoiselle,
"lies in the way you get
from one note to the other."
Do re mi fa so la ti do
You'd rather read and escape
this unmanageable place.

You asked me, "How did you keep the secret?"
as we stood in the kitchen
the morning after she died, and for the first time
I recognized myself,
the organizer of deceptions
so hastily thrown up between us.
I wept, then, because you understood.

Maps

In his cluttered room, socks and comics
on the floor, a Metro map spreads its tangles
of blue and red and green above the bed.
On Saturdays he travels to unexplored stations,
returns and circles them in triumph.
"Do you walk in the neighborhoods?" I ask.

No, he just wants to follow the mind
that worked the system out, to play
the boards where flashing lights
spell the routes to destinations.

Together we chant the names
of my favorite stations: *Gaité, Abbesses,*
Bonne-Nouvelle. He's gone where I have never been...
Michel-Ange-Molitor...Eglise de Pantin...
exotic urban ports of call.

But Agnès scolds, "Madame doesn't understand.
Paris is dangerous. There are men who harm
boys. He shouldn't be alone."

Give him one more element to fear? Never.
Looking in his eyes, I wonder how he sees
the city I worshipped at twenty, idolized
like a first lover.

"Don't worry," he says unexpectedly one day,
"I have a map and I don't talk to anyone."

Practice

The movers, swift and kind,
forgive our meager possessions.
"You want this, and this?" they ask, holding up
each object. Before I can nod, it is wrapped,
even a candle stub, quick into the box.
Light grows bolder in the rooms;
emptiness rushes in; where the rug lay,
patches of sun stamp our departure.

My shopping cart with its plaid basket
will never again attract boastful vendors
at the market—
Look, look at my beautiful oranges!

Going home: the children test their joy
again and again, and I practice, too, tasting
the blood orange, violet-red,
bitter on my tongue.

Afternoon

Crossing the Champs de Mars,
gravel shifting under my feet,
I look toward the dome
of the Ecole Militaire. Its gilded pomp
obscures the fact of barracks
where men live and learn to kill.

Summer has refurbished the umbrella trees.
At my back, the Eiffel Tower
looms like a reconstructed dinosaur.
Some children in blue smocks,
legs skinny as sandpipers',
run singing from their mothers.
The air leaves my lungs:
she will never see this with me—
it is three o'clock—
and I know.

Acknowledgments

Grateful acknowledgement is made to the following publications in which these poems first appeared: *The New Yorker*: "Translated;" *GRAND STREET*: "When," "Nowhere," "Holding On."

Special thanks to Miriam Goodman and Marnie Mueller for their long time encouragement; to Pamela Alexander, Jessica Stone, and Geraldine Zetzel for critical readings; and to Kathi Aguero, Suzanne E. Berger, Erica Funkhouser, Kinereth Gensler, Helena Minton, and Connie Veenendaal for their support.

Alice James Books gratefully acknowledges support from the University of Maine at Farmington and the National Endowment for the Arts.

Alice James Books gratefully acknowledges the support of the Jane Kenyon Memorial Fund in inaugurating the Jane Kenyon Chapbook Award Series.

Recent Titles from Alice James Books

Doug Anderson, *The Moon Reflected Fire*
Robert Cording, *Heavy Grace*
Deborah DeNicola, *Where Divinity Begins*
Theodore Deppe, *The Wanderer King*
B. H. Fairchild, *The Art of the Lathe*
Rita Gabis, *The Wild Field*
Kinereth Gensler, *Journey Fruit*
Forrest Hamer, *Call and Response*
Cynthia Huntington, *We Have Gone to the Beach*
Sharon Kraus, *Generation*
E. J. Miller Laino, *Girl Hurt*
Richard McCann, *Ghost Letters*
Nora Mitchell, *Proofreading the Histories*
Carol Potter, *Upside Down in the Dark*
Adrienne Su, *Middle Kingdom*
Lisa Sewall, *The Way Out*
Ellen Watson, *We Live in Bodies*